How To Live A Life Of Blessing

*A practical guide to walking
in the blessing of God*

BARRY YOUNG

Print ISBN: 978-1-54398-937-3
eBook ISBN: 978-1-54398-938-0

DEDICATION

*This book is dedicated to the pastors I have had
the blessing of serving. Thank you Rev. Robert
Fredericks, Dr. Ray Brewer, Rev. Bill Newby,
Dr. Dan Carroll, Dr. Linda Jones, Rev. Todd
Blansit, Rev. Brad Oyler, Rev. Kevin Smith and
Rev. Matt Purkey. I have had the blessing to
work with or for each of these pastors in some
capacity. I love them and appreciate their deep
influence on my life. Although they are all
incredible preachers, the greatest message they
preach is the way they live their lives.*

ACKNOWLEDGMENT

I deeply love and appreciate these incredible people for their support, wisdom, and godly direction. They have been invaluable to my life!

Serving Pastors Partners: I would like to thank all of our ministry supporters and giving partners. We could not do what we do without your prayers and support. The constant flow of genuine love and encouragement you give inspires us to do what God has called us to do. You are making an eternal difference. We deeply love you and thank God for you.

Strategos International: I want to give special thanks to Vaughn and Glenda Baker as well as Mark and Leanda Warren. It is such a blessing and honor to work with them and Strategos International. Because of their efforts, countless lives have been saved and protected through the many trainings and programs Strategos provides worldwide.

My family: I can't begin to express how grateful I am for the overwhelming blessing and encouragement of my family. I am so rich from the amazing amount of love and support I have received from them. I love and appreciate you!

Kelly Young: I am grateful for the love, support, and wisdom of my wife. Her hard work on this project and all the projects I do is priceless. I am so thankful God has allowed me to be ministry partners with her, and more importantly, life partners. I love you!

TABLE OF CONTENTS

FACTS ABOUT YOUR LIFE

Science can't answer the three most important questions we have in life. Where did we come from? Why are we here? Where will we go when we die?

Friend, it isn't an accident that this book is in your hand. One day you are going to die, and so will I. Are you walking with God? Are you right with God? Have you asked his Son, Jesus Christ, into your life? There is absolutely no way you, by yourself, can earn eternal life! The Bible clearly states in Romans 3:23, "All have sinned." The Bible also clearly states in Romans 6:23, "For the wages of sin is death." We will all die, and if we do not receive the gift of eternal life found only in Jesus, we have nothing to look forward to but physical death and then an eternity separated from God. There is, however, hope!

PRAYER OF SALVATION

Having eternal life with God is not about a religion, it is not about a specific church, and it is certainly not about the efforts of man. Having eternal life is about a person, Jesus Christ.

If you would like to receive Jesus Christ as Lord, he can save you, forgive you, heal you, love you, and most importantly, give you eternal life. The Bible says in Romans 10:9-10, "If you confess with your mouth the Lord Jesus and believe in your heart that God has raised him from the dead, you will be saved. For with the heart one believes unto righteousness, and with the mouth confession is made unto salvation." If you would like to receive eternal life, would you pray this prayer?

> *Lord Jesus, right now I call on your name. I ask you to be the Lord of my life. I ask you to forgive me for all of my sins. I confess with my mouth and I believe in my heart that you died on the cross and rose from the grave. I receive your love and your salvation.*

Friend, if you prayed that prayer in faith, you are now a Christian. If you are not in a Bible-believing church, start attending one now. As believers, we need one another. If you prayed this prayer, would you contact our ministry at www.servingpastors.com? We would love to hear your story.

INTRODUCTION

I don't know one Christian who doesn't want to live a blessed life. However, sadly a majority of Christians are not genuinely living the life of blessing God desires for them. Living a life of blessing is not about being money focused. A wise man once said, "Money never made a man rich" and this saying is so true! Instead, living a life of blessing is about being God focused.

Would you consider that God wants you radically and outrageously blessed? Reflect on the following Old and New Testament scriptures that demonstrate the blessing of God:

- Jeremiah 29:11 "For I know the thoughts that I think toward you, says the Lord, thoughts of peace and not of evil, to give you a future and a hope."

- John 10:10 "I (Jesus) have come that they may have life, and that they may have it more abundantly."

- Exodus 14:14 "The Lord will fight for you, and you shall hold your peace."

- Romans 8:31 "If God is for us, who can be against us?"

- Deuteronomy 28:13 "And the Lord will make you the head and not the tail; you shall be above only, and not be beneath."

- Luke 1:37 "For with God nothing will be impossible."

- Isaiah 54:17 "No weapon formed against you shall prosper."

- John 3:16 "For God so loved the world that He gave His only begotten Son, that whoever believes in Him should not perish but have everlasting life."

The Word of God makes it abundantly clear that God wants you blessed! So, what does it mean to live a life of blessing? It is doing what God has called you to do, being who God has called you to be, and having what God has called you to have. Let me repeat that statement again. Living a life of blessing is doing what God has called you to do, being who God has called you to be, and having what God has called you to have! Let's briefly examine those three statements:

Doing what God has called you to do. No amount of money can truly make you happy if you are not doing what God has called you to do. Unfortunately, many Christians spend their lives doing something they were never called to do. There are many reasons why Christians get their lives out of the sweet spot God has for them. Some chase money, some are lazy, some won't consider the cost, some have committed sins they think disqualify them from God's plan, and some have believed a lie from the devil. Living a life of blessing is living a life where you are doing exactly what God has created and called you to do.

Being who God has called you to be. God will never call you to be somebody else; he will always call you to be you. If your faith is in Jesus, you are a son or daughter of God. You are a King's kid. Hollywood, social media, and this culture are creating false images to define success. The vast majority of people lack confidence and struggle with insecurities. The root cause of this issue is that most people just don't think they measure up. This thought is such a lie and a demonic attack from the devil and hell itself. When you know who you are in Jesus, you understand your worth is not derived from how you look, or how much money you make, or the position/title you hold. Your worth comes from the fact that Jesus Christ, the very Son of God, thought you were so valuable that he died on the cross for you. If Jesus Christ cherishes you so much that he was willing to lay down his life for you, how much more valuable can you be? Living a life of blessing is living a life where you become the person God wants you to be. Many Christians hide behind a mask and aren't happy with who they really are. God wants you to be who he has called you to be.

Having what God wants you to have. First and foremost, God wants you to receive his Son, Jesus, and have eternal life with him. There is nothing more important in all the earth than for you to have a personal relationship with Jesus and to have the reassurance that your sins are forgiven. I believe this truth so strongly that in every book I write, it must have the plan and prayer of salvation in it. However, God not only wants your soul to be saved, he also desires that your family, friends, and coworkers be saved. God also wants you to have joy, peace, and for you to walk in authority and love. If you have all that God wants you to have, it doesn't matter how much money is in your bank account — you are blessed!

As you read this book, I want the following truth to be cemented in your spirit, God wants you blessed! God wants you blessed! One more time, God wants you blessed! However, if you want to live a life of blessing, you have to position yourself to be blessed, and this book is dedicated to helping you do just that!

We are going to look at a small, yet powerful story found in Mark 11:20-24. In these verses are treasure troves of wisdom on how to position our lives to receive the blessings God wants to give us. The ultimate authority on blessing is Jesus. As we study this story, I hope these truths overwhelm you and help you position yourself to be blessed.

I pray over you and every person who reads this book this simple prayer:

"Lord, help every reader of this book to do everything you want them to do, to be everything you want them to be, and lastly, to have everything you want them to have. In Jesus name I pray, Amen!"

I love you. Be blessed!

Barry

1

YOU SPEAK CURSES, YOU GET CURSES

"The fig tree which you cursed has withered away."

Mark 11:21

Words are the key to this world and the universe itself. Consider for a moment that there was no universe until God created it. How did God create the universe? Genesis 1:3 has the answer and it states, "Then God said, 'Let there be light'; and there was light." God used words to create this world and everything in it. How did Jesus stop the winds and waves from harming or possibly killing the disciples? Matthew 8:26 states, "Then he (Jesus) arose and rebuked the winds and the sea, and there was a great calm." How do people get saved? The Bible says in Romans 10:9, "That if you confess with your mouth the Lord Jesus and believe in your heart that God has raised him from the dead, you will be saved." Wow! God used words to create the universe. Jesus used words to perform ministry and protect people. We use words through faith to become believers.

The Bible says in Proverbs 18:21, "Death and life are in the power of the tongue, and those who love it will eat its fruit." Understanding the power of our words is so vital for every believer!

Before I go any further, let me acknowledge that there has been a tremendous amount of false teaching on this area of the gospel. Some believers have taken scriptures out of context to create a gospel where God is nothing more than a divine Santa Claus. There have been Christians who try to use the Word of God to perform their own will. Please understand that the Bible does not conform to us, but we conform to the Bible. Because there has been so much false teaching on the power of words, many pastors steer clear of teaching on this subject and that is exactly what the devil wants.

I believe the Bible teaches we should simply agree with God. The Bible is God's Word and we should agree with what it says. Using a scripture out of context to try to force God to give me fifteen 747 jets for my ministry is not the gospel, it is foolishness. However, let's suppose someone has sinned and then repented to God, but they still feel guilty for their sin. What should they do? They need to believe 1 John 1:9 which states, "If we confess our sins, he is faithful and just to forgive us our sins and to cleanse us from all unrighteousness." There is power when we read God's Word, agree with what it says, and speak it over our lives. In Matthew 4, the devil comes to tempt Jesus. Every time the devil spoke tempting words, Jesus responded in Matthew 4:4, 4:7, and 4:10 with a simple phrase, "It is written." When tempted, Jesus himself quoted the Word of God to the devil. Speaking the Word was the way that Jesus dealt with temptation. It worked for him and it will also work for us! So please hear my heart, we aren't supposed to stand on our fleshly desires, we are supposed to stand on the Word of God that is taken in context.

We read in Mark 11:21, "The fig tree which you cursed has withered away." This scripture teaches us that if you speak curses, you will get curses. This statement was true then, and it is still true today. How did the fig tree die? Curses spoken over the tree caused the tree to wither away. I am sure if I asked you to remember a time when someone spoke mean and hurtful words over you, that you could probably recall numerous times when that has happened in your life. Words hurt. The old saying goes, "Sticks and stones may break my bones, but names will never hurt me." This phrase is true in that names won't hurt you; names can destroy you! How many young people today are committing suicide because the devil has told them they aren't worth anything? How many adults have walked away from their dreams because the devil lied to them and told them their dreams couldn't come true?

Watch the Way You Talk About Yourself

Your identity doesn't come from your education, bank account, title/position, or outer appearance. The only way you can have peace with who you are is when your identity comes from God. God says in Romans 8:37, "We are more than conquerors through him who loved us." The word conqueror means to be a champion. God is saying you are a champion. You might not feel or look like one, but if God says you are a champion, then you are one!

If you make a statement such as, "I can't do it", then more than likely you won't be able to do it. If you say, "I won't win", then you probably won't win. If you declare to others, "I won't graduate", then there is a high possibility you won't graduate. There is power in your words. The Bible even teaches that we are saved by our confession, or words we declare with our mouth. Look at Romans 10:9, "If you confess with your mouth the Lord Jesus and believe in your heart that God has raised him from the dead, you will be saved." The words we speak are so powerful!

Perhaps you have been your own worst enemy without even realizing it. What words are you declaring over your life? What words are you declaring over your future? What words are you declaring over your relationships? We can only speak two types of messages over our lives. We can speak life, or we can speak death.

Many years ago, when it was a big deal to have a circus come into town, one of the favorite attractions was watching the elephants perform. How could the circus trainers contain these massive beasts as they traveled throughout the country from week to week? Basically, when a circus elephant was born, the trainer would place a small metal cuff around the baby elephant's rear leg. Then, a small rope or chain was attached to the cuff, and that rope/chain would be connected to a tent stake that was driven into the ground. When the baby elephant grew in size and weighed thousands of pounds, the circus trainers could still contain the elephant the exact same way as when they were babies. How could a cuff and rope/chain that was merely attached to a tent stake contain this enormous elephant? Basically, it was all the elephant understood! The truth is that the fully-grown elephant had the power to pull out one hundred tent stakes from the ground! However, since all the elephant knew was bondage, when it became fully grown and powerful, the elephant still stayed in bondage.

That story of the elephant is a picture of a born-again Christian who struggles to strip off their former nature and ways of thinking. When you receive Christ as Lord, you have God's power to walk in freedom. Galatians 5:1 says, "Stand fast therefore in the liberty by which Christ has made us free, and do not be entangled again with a yoke of bondage." Friend, you are free! But, in order to have freedom, you have to agree with God's Word and walk in the freedom he has given you. It is time for you to start pulling some tent stakes out of the ground!

I am begging you today, speak life! Speak life over your job! Speak life over your marriage! Speak life over your finances! Speak life over your family! It doesn't take any spiritual courage or character to speak death about all the negative and painful events of life. However, it does take spiritual bravery to speak life when we encounter trials and lack in our lives.

Watch the Way You Talk About Others

It is so easy to put others down! Oftentimes, we might hear someone else speaking negatively about another person, and then we jump in and start speaking hurtful words too. Friend, when you choose to speak badly about another person, you are sowing seeds you don't want to reap. The Bible clearly teaches the law of sowing and reaping. If you speak negative words over others, you are sowing negativity. If you speak slander over others, you are sowing slander. If you speak lies over others, you are sowing lies.

I have learned a principle over the years. It is always easier to tear a church down than to build it up. It is always simpler to tear people down than it is to build them up. My experience in life is that often the easier road is actually the more difficult road to travel in the long run. Don't let the devil use you to speak death over others. Please consider this thought: If you are speaking ill over godly people, you have allowed yourself to become a tool of the enemy. Every person has faults, issues and shortcomings. It doesn't take an anointing from God to spot other people's deficiencies. However, it does take an anointing from God to help others overcome their issues.

There is a simple phrase God spoke to me years ago and this word changed my life: S*ave your bullets for the devil.* Basically, this statement means to use your words, influence, and life to tear down the devil's kingdom, not God's. When we attack other Christians with our words or actions, we are allowing the enemy to use us to hurt others.

If you listen to the sermons I have preached and read the books I have written, I refuse to speak/write negatively about another person or church. It isn't my job to tear churches or people down, but instead, my calling is to build churches and people up. Do we need to stand up for what is right and stand on God's Word as the source of life and truth? Absolutely yes! We need to make sure we never water down the gospel. However, what sets people free is not preaching about what other people or churches are doing wrong. What sets people free is preaching about Jesus dying on the cross and rising from the grave! What sets people free is being filled with the Holy Spirit. What sets people free is surrendering to the will of God for their life!

Let me give you one last word of caution. If your closest friends and family put others down when you are with them, you can be certain that they will put you down when you are away from them. Embrace speaking hope! Embrace speaking life! Embrace speaking and preaching the gospel of Jesus Christ!

2

YOU SPEAK BLESSINGS, YOU GET BLESSINGS

"But believes that those things he says will be done, he will have whatever he says."

Mark 11:23

In Mark 11:23, Jesus gives us an incredible promise when he says, "But believes that those things he says will be done, he will have whatever he says." Wow! What an amazing and miraculous promise this is from Jesus! Notice that what we say is directly tied into what we receive. Also, there are no limits on this promise!

If you begin to speak blessings, it will change your world. People love to be around positive people, yet find it draining to be around those who are negative. You can't have a positive life and speak with a negative mouth. Not only will others enjoy being around us when we speak blessings, but when we speak affirmative words of faith, we are forming a supernatural partnership with God! When was the last time you spoke faith and blessings over a situation that seemed hopeless?

Speaking blessings is contagious. Just like when one person begins to complain, others start complaining. The same can be true when one person starts to speak blessings, others jump in and begin to build each other up with encouraging words. It just takes one man or woman to change the entire atmosphere at a job, school, church, or home with the positive words they choose to speak.

Proclaim, declare, and talk about the blessings of God!

Begin to Believe Your Life Can Be Great

God designed the born-again Christian to win. Have you ever considered that God truly designed you to be great and to do remarkable things? The Bible clearly says in Genesis 1:27 that, "God created man in his own image." You may need to put this book down for a few moments just to ponder this thought that you were made in the image of the Creator of the universe. Every believer in Jesus was created to walk in power.

Do you know how the devil places people in bondage? The moment we believe a lie from the devil is when the handcuffs of bondage start to be placed on us. We can't debate the devil's lies because we don't have the power to argue with him. However, we do have the power to believe in and speak the Word of God. When you speak and believe the scriptures in the Bible, you will stop the devil in his tracks every time. The devil can't harm you; all he can do is give you suggestions. Bondage starts when we take him up on those suggestions.

One of the quickest ways you can make sure that your life's vision is small is to let other people dream for you. This notion is so common in our culture today. Many people on this planet are doing things with their lives they don't actually want to do. Regardless of how much a friend, family member, or even your pastor loves you, don't let them dream and vision cast for your life! Instead, seek God's wisdom because he has incredible and awesome plans in store for you!

Let me share a story with you about an escape artist from many years ago who had performed numerous dramatic escapes. One day, the local police department contacted him about a jail cell they believed he could not break out of. This challenge was all the escape artist needed because it motivated him to prove the police wrong. The next day he went to the police station where they escorted him into the jail cell, and then slammed the door shut behind him. Once in the cell, he attempted to pick the lock, but that didn't work. He then tried to take the hinges off the doors but that also failed. He made attempts to squeeze through the bars, but his efforts were unsuccessful. Finally, in frustration, he slammed his head against the cell door and said, "I give up." When his head knocked into the door, it suddenly opened. The police put him in a cell that had never been locked in the first place. This story is a representation of how many of us can be as believers. We live as though we are locked in a prison cell, but the truth is the door is actually unlocked. As a son or daughter of God, Jesus died on the cross and rose from the grave so you could come out of prisons of anxiety, fear, and guilt. You are free! Speak the Word of God over your life!

Begin to believe your life can be great! Know in your heart that God wants to use you to change the world. Embrace the reality that you have a supernatural, divine purpose on the inside of you just waiting to come out. There will always be wonder-working power active in your life when you simply agree with what God says about you. Don't agree with what the devil or your own flesh says about you. Agree with what God declares about you. Joyce Meyer says it best, "You can be pitiful, or you can be powerful, but you can't be both."

Begin to Introduce a New You

When you begin to meditate on and speak the written Word of God over your life, things will begin to shift. You will walk in more power. You will walk in more authority. And you will walk in more of God's blessing. At this point, God may be calling you to introduce a new you. Perhaps God is calling you to be a new leader. Maybe he has called you to be a new and improved spouse. Or possibly, God might be pulling at your heartstrings to start some new ministry for his kingdom. Whatever God is speaking to you about oftentimes when you get exposed to the blessings of God in a radical way, God will desire for you to introduce a new you.

After the battle with Goliath, a little shepherd boy named David was introduced as a great warrior. After spending time in jail and then being released by Pharaoh, a lowly prisoner named Joseph was introduced as second-in-command over his entire nation. After denying Jesus publicly but then encountering the power of the Holy Spirit, the deserter named Peter was introduced as the head of the church. God wants to introduce a new you!

Don't worry about what others think! You can't encounter God in a radical way and not be changed. Jesus did not die for you to be a better person. Jesus died so the dead would be made alive again. When you start believing and then speaking the truth of God, the areas of your life where God wants to do something new will start to bubble up on the inside of you. Do not give in to worry. As a believer you have the choice and the power to say no to worry. Consider John 14:1, "Do not let your hearts be troubled." Jesus is saying here that you have the power to determine if your heart will be troubled or not.

Do you want to be weak or powerful? If you want to be weak, repeat what the devil says about you. If you want to be strong, repeat what God says about you.

When we speak negative and hurtful words over and over again, the pain will go deeper. However, when we speak God's life-giving words over our lives, his power gets rooted into our hearts and lives.

Consider this truth: what you yield to, you will be full of. When you yield to bitterness, you will be full of bitterness. When you yield to anger, you will be full of anger. But also, when you yield to joy, you will be full of joy. When you yield to the power of God, you will be filled with God's power. When you yield to the peace of God you will be filled with God's peace.

Today, I challenge you to pursue God's dreams for your life, get God's blessings and walk in them! God wants to bless your life. You can't have a positive life and a negative outlook. Read and meditate on the promises in God's Word and then declare those scriptures over your life establishing boundaries of blessing. Declaring the Word over your life is like having a supernatural GPS that keeps you on the righteous path of God! Reflect on Mark 11:23 one more time, "But believes that those things he says will be done, he will have whatever he says." Use your words as weapons to defeat the enemy and his attacks against your life. Speak blessings!

3

YOU CANNOT LET THE CURRENT FACTS INTERFERE WITH THE FUTURE RESULTS

*"Whoever says to this mountain,
'Be removed and be cast into the sea.'"*

Mark 11:23

It is not how you start the race that counts, but it is how you finish! Some of the greatest sports champions started in last before they moved into first. Many of boxers have been knocked down only to get up and become the victor. Consider these words from former boxing champion Mike Tyson, "Everyone has a plan until they get punched in the face."

Has life ever punched you in the face? If you are going to live a life of blessing, you have to be able to take a few punches. Sadly, you may have to take on more punches than you would like. Basically, life is not fair and nowhere in the Bible does God declare that life is impartial. The devil is going to try his best to stop you from living in blessing. John 10:10 declares, "The thief does not come except to steal, and to kill, and to destroy", and that is exactly what the devil wants to do to you.

Sometimes we will be up against what seems like mountains. When we face a mountain, we can either choose to turn around and give up, or we can speak to the mountain according to Mark 11:23. Would you step out in faith and speak to your mountain?

We may not have control over the punches that life throws our way, but would you consider this thought? My response is my responsibility. God commands us to love our spouses, honor our parents, and to love one another. However, sometimes our relationships can go sideways. There is one key concept that can help your relationships if you will receive it: My response is my responsibility! Your spouse or friends can't do things to make you respond in a hurtful or ungodly way. You are the one who controls how you will respond. If you truly want healthy relationships, you need to respond to others in love even when you don't feel like it and especially when they don't deserve it!

The Bible says in Matthew 5:45, "He sends rain on the just and on the unjust." When you encounter an unfair circumstance in your life, you only have two choices. You can either become a victim or a student. The victim starts grumbling, complaining, and blaming other people for what has happened to them. The student tries to understand how they can grow and learn from the unfortunate painful situation. When life is unfair to you, will you choose to be a victim or a student? Those who make the tough choice to be a student are the ones who change the world! You cannot let the current facts interfere with the future results.

Don't Focus on What You're Currently Struggling With

The devil wants you to be fixated on your problems, and he wants you constantly thinking, talking, and reminding yourself about all the issues you are facing. Sometimes uninformed but well-intentioned believers will try to get you focused on all aspects of your trials. However, focusing on your problems never brings solutions; it only brings misery!

When you ruminate about your troubles, you are unable to think about the goodness of God. Placing focus on all your problems will bog you down and provide an ungodly distraction that will unfortunately cause you to miss God's blessings.

Talking about problems may seem like a good idea at first. For example, professional counselors spend time helping their clients open up to freely discuss their problems. These counseling sessions can seem helpful at first, but many times those same clients struggle to move forward after unpacking all their problems to a counselor. Please understand that counseling can be considered beneficial if it is based on the Word of God and empowered and led by the Spirit of God. However, counseling that is void of the presence of Jesus will never really set a person free. Can you imagine if someone used a damp mop to clean a messy floor, but then never wrung out the dirty mop with cleanser? This picture is a depiction of what counseling is like without Jesus. When we just talk about life's problems without Jesus, we simply just move the dirt around without getting cleaned.

Many years ago, my mom was told she had cancer. She had tests and scans done, and there was no doubt that cancer was invading her body. She had two options; either focus on the cancer or focus on God. Thankfully, she chose to focus on God. Every day when I came home from school, I found my mom sitting in her chair reading the Bible. Every time I came out of my room, she was reading her Bible. When I came home after playing with friends, guess what she was doing? You guessed it, reading her Bible! She didn't ignore the fact that she had cancer, but instead of focusing on the cancer, she chose to focus on her God. This year, my mom will be cancer-free for 30 years and will celebrate her 81st birthday! The bottom line is that you can't let the current facts interfere with the future results! The fact was that my mom had cancer, but the truth is that God healed her, and the future result is that she is alive today!

Thinking about life's problems and talking about life's hurts are just tools the devil uses to remind us of the pains of life. However, God has a different plan. Philippians 3:13 says, "Forgetting those things which are behind." Don't focus on the trials you are currently struggling with. You can't focus on the problem, if it is to be solved. You have to focus on the answer.

Focus on the Victory That is to Come

Once our mind, eyes, and mouth stop focusing on the problems we are struggling with, we can then focus on the victory that is to come. Too many times we live our lives according to the nickname of Missouri, which is the Show-Me-State. When we operate under the premise that we must first see in order to believe, we will never have the full blessings of God!

To live a life of blessing, you have to first believe, and then you will see! 2 Corinthians 5:7 says, "For we walk by faith, not by sight." Many times, we find ourselves doing the opposite and walk by sight and not by faith. Walking by sight will only let you have natural dreams, but if you walk by faith, you will experience God's supernatural dreams and victories for your life.

Too often in prayer we make a big mistake in spending all our time telling God how big our problems are. It is important to share your heart with God and tell him about your struggles. However, if we are not careful, we can get to the place where our prayer time turns into a time of complaining. Instead of telling God how big your problems are, you need to start telling your problems how big your God is! This one act can start unleashing the blessing of God in your life.

Pastor Douglas Cline once told me, "Nothing changes if nothing changes." Wow! That hit me like a ton of bricks. Nothing will change in your life until you change! If you want something in your life to change then you have to be willing to make changes. We need to stop focusing on all the setbacks in our life and instead, focus on the victory and power that God promises to all believers.

What are your eyes fixated on today? When you face a problem or obstacle in your life, you need to ask yourself this question: Am I focused on the problem or am I focused on the answer? Colossians 3:2 says, "Set your mind on things above, not on things on the earth." You can live a life of blessing if you will refuse to focus on what you're struggling with and choose to focus on the victory that is to come. You can't change your life until you change your thinking!

4

YOU CANNOT ASK SMALL
AND RECEIVE BIG

*"Therefore I say to you, whatever things you
ask when you pray, believe that you receive them,
and you will have them."*

Mark 11:24

One of the biggest mistakes we make in prayer is that we pray too small. As believers, we oftentimes pray through the lens of our limited power. Instead, we should pray through the lens of God's limitless power! Jesus makes a bold and radical promise in Mark 11:24, "Therefore I say to you, whatever things you ask when you pray, believe that you receive them, and you will have them." However, this promise will not become a reality in our lives until we actually start to believe and act on it.

You can't ask small and receive big! If you ask small, you will receive small. If you ask little, you will receive little. If you ask tiny, you will receive tiny. However, thank God the opposite is true as well. If you ask big, you will receive big. If you ask large, you will receive large. If you ask miraculous, you will receive miraculous. How are you praying? Are you asking small or are you asking big?

Many times, believers can get discouraged because they aren't seeing dramatic results in their prayer time and life. I have seen Christians who ask small, but then hope to receive big. This kind of prayer life is not successful, nor will it ever be successful. Jesus saw the lame healed, the blind receive sight, and the dead come back to life. He received big because he asked and believed big. We have to do things the way Jesus did if we want to receive big. If we do things our way, we will never get the same results as Jesus. Ask big!

Are you believing God for radical and outrageous results? If not, start now! Begin to believe God for the things the devil has told you are impossible. Start to believe God for things that your human senses don't believe can happen. God specializes in accomplishing what we don't think is possible. The reality is that the majority of the time we will get what we pray for when we pray in line with God's Word. You don't get saved according to Romans 10:9-10 until you step out in faith and believe in Jesus and his resurrection. Your name does not get written in the Lamb's book of life until you call on the name of the Lord not to modify your behavior, but to bring your dead soul to life.

The Bible is full of amazing miracles that took place. However, big prayers were prayed before many of those miracles materialized. Pray bigger. Ask larger. Step out in faith and ask for things that nobody else in your world will believe God for!

Are You Limiting Yourself?

The prayers of God's people can move mountains. But many times, we limit ourselves. If we are not careful, our thinking can limit us from receiving all that God has for us. There is no way to have a positive life if we have a negative mindset. Sometimes we can be our own worst enemies. How many times have we seen great men of God in the Bible trip over the way they use their words, faith, and prayers? For example, we see David give in to lust, Noah getting drunk, and Peter cursing onlookers. We can also limit ourselves just like these men of faith.

However, God is an unlimited resource. Luke 1:37 says, "For with God nothing will be impossible." God can set you free from depression. God can deliver you and set you free from low self-esteem. God can give you freedom from any addiction. You can live a life of blessing! But you can't live a life of blessing if you are limiting yourself.

Many years ago, Walt Disney had a dream for something bigger after he had built Disneyland in California. His dream was to create Disney World and to build it in Florida. Walt Disney tragically died before the actual completion of this project in Orlando, Florida. Nevertheless, the world's largest amusement park was finally completed.

At the opening ceremony of the park, the new CEO for the Walt Disney Corporation, Michael Eisner was interviewed. The interviewer asked Eisner, "Wouldn't it have been great if Walt Disney had lived long enough to see Disney World?" Michael Eisner had a powerful response, "He did see it, and that is why it is here today." Friend, the Bible says in 2 Corinthians 5:7, "For we walk by faith, not by sight." Walt Disney saw what others could not see. If you want your life blessed, don't wait for somebody else to see it. Look through the eyes of faith and see your life, marriage, family, and finances blessed.

Faith is not believing God can. Faith is believing God will. It doesn't take faith to say, "I believe God *can* forgive me." It does take faith to say, "God *will* and has forgiven me." Please keep in mind that everything we pray and think needs to come from the Word of God, and in context! Psalm 103:3 says, "He forgives all your iniquities." I don't care what sins you may have committed. If you go to God and ask for his forgiveness in the name of Jesus, you will be forgiven. We simply want to agree with what God says about us!

We will never accomplish great things for God if we can't see them becoming reality through the eyes of faith. We will never change neighborhoods and nations if we only trust what we see. We have to trust what we know. We need to have big dreams in a big God with big faith. Are you like Walt Disney having dreams of something so big that others simply can't imagine it? Here is good news; your dreams can never be too big for God!

Are You Limiting God?

The only force that can stop God from moving in your life is YOU! Joshua 24:15 declares, "Choose for yourselves this day whom you will serve." As much as God desires to bless us, he will not force us to be blessed. As much as God desires to do great and incredible things in our lives, he will not override our choices and force us to walk in his blessing.

If you choose to be miserable, God will let you be miserable. If you choose to be broke, God will let you be broke. Our doubt and unbelief can instantly stop the supernatural power of God from flowing in our lives. We can limit God!

There are several ways to limit God, but one of the primary ways we limit his blessing in our lives is when we don't submit to authority. We shouldn't say to God, "This is what I am doing, I want you to bless it." Instead, our prayer should be, "Lord, tell me what you are blessing, and I will do that." Have you ever jumped feet first into something, and then expected God to bless what you were doing? Psalm 127:1 proclaims, "Unless the Lord builds the house, they labor in vain who build it." We can't build what God has not inspired.

We need to submit to God, pray in the will of God, and believe the plan of God. You might be asking the question; how do I know God's will? God's will is his Word. God's will is the Bible. We have to pray, think, believe, and speak according to what the Bible says.

We can also limit God by not submitting to the human authority he has placed over us. Romans 13:1 says: "Let every soul be subject to the governing authorities. For there is no authority except from God." Wow! Did you catch what this scripture is stating? The authorities who rule over us have been established and placed there by God. You will never get promoted in life until you submit to the authority God has placed over you. I have had pastors ask me what qualities they should look for when trying to find a good leader. I always tell them they need to find **FAT** leaders, which means:

Faithful. Great leaders are always dependable in what they do. There are times when pastors will attempt to put talented people in leadership hoping this will make them faithful. If people are not faithful without a title, they won't be faithful with one. I would rather have a less talented, faithful person on my team than one who was talented, yet unfaithful. A person will never be fruitful until they are faithful.

Available. A true leader is one who is always there to help and serve when needed. If you have an incredibly talented person on your team, but they don't show up to meetings or events, that is of no use to your church or organization. Nothing can replace a person who always shows up and serves when you need them the most!

Teachable. Have you ever been around someone who already thought they knew everything? These kinds of people are not enjoyable to be around. When a person understands that they still have a lot to learn, they can change the world.

Friend, if you want to be promoted in life be a person who is FAT. I promise if you will be faithful, available, and teachable to God and the authorities God has placed over your life, you will get promoted. You can't help but advance in life when you are FAT.

We can even see the roots of the importance of submitting to authority in the Ten Commandments. Exodus 20:12 says, "Honor your father and your mother, that your days may be long upon the land." Submission is vital in our marriages, our prayer lives, our work relationships, our families, and in every area of our lives. When you submit to God and the authorities that God has placed over you, you are now positioning yourself to be blessed!

5

YOU MUST PUT YOUR FAITH IN GOD

*"Jesus answered and said to them,
'Have faith in God.'"*

Mark 11:22

I believe in preaching faith. I believe in speaking faith. I believe in declaring in faith. However, to have faith in faith is powerless because it is nothing more than a religion created by man! However, when you put your faith in God hell trembles and demons shake.

Our faith must be in God if it is to carry any weight and power. There is no supernatural power without faith in God. There is no resurrection of Jesus without faith in God. There is no New Testament church without faith in God. There are no salvations and life transformations without faith in God.

Sometimes as believers, we can put our faith in a great preacher, powerful ministry, or an incredible movement that God has birthed. All of these things are wonderful blessings. But our faith has to be squarely set on God. Jesus tells his followers in Mark 11:22, "Have faith in God." I believe Jesus is stating this truth because sometimes we can easily get distracted. At times we can start with God, but finish in our flesh. Our faith must be resolutely in God.

Consider the scenario that someone needs a life-threatening surgery. Imagine if they survived and were made completely healthy again. How silly would it be for that person to start thanking the scalpel?! Can you imagine them writing a thank you note to the scalpel? This notion is absurd! The reason this depiction is crazy is because the scalpel is a tool. Yes, God uses preachers, ministries, and churches but ultimately those are all tools that God uses to heal people's lives. Friend, our faith has to be in God, not man!

Believe God for His Promises

What does it mean to have faith in God? Having faith in God means that we believe and act upon the promises in his Word. Here are five cardinal promises that every believer must stand on:

- Romans 10:13 "For whoever calls on the name of the Lord shall be saved."

Thank God for the truth of this verse. No matter where you come from or where you have been, if you call on the Lord you will be saved. The devil tries to lie to new and rooted believers by telling them they are not saved. If you have called on the name of the Lord, don't believe the devil! We need to stand firm on and believe this promise from God.

- 1 John 1:9 "If we confess our sins, he is faithful and just to forgive us our sins."

We can never have peace with God or in this life until we have the knowledge and assurance that every sin we have committed is forgiven. Sometimes receiving the forgiveness of God can seem too good to be true. But the truth is that Jesus paid our debt in full when he died on the cross. He died so we could be forgiven for every sin ever committed in the past, present and future. Confess and repent of your sins to God and you will be forgiven. You need to stand firm on this precious and powerful promise especially when the devil tries to make you feel guilty for past sins.

- Philippians 4:13 "I can do all things through Christ who strengthens me."

Aside from the word *Christ* in this verse, the most important word is *all*. God is communicating in his Word that you can do all things through Christ. Have you ever noticed that throughout God's Word, he is trying to encourage his followers to get their faith up? God wants those who have decided to serve him to believe for big things! All things are possible. Nothing big, nothing miraculous, and nothing world-changing ever takes place unless it is through Christ!

- Psalm 147:3 "He heals the brokenhearted and binds up their wounds."

We are all broken. Each of us have hurts, habits, and bondages that we deal with every day. We can't find healing in ourselves or in others. We can only find lasting healing for life's most painful events in Jesus. Now, God often uses people to heal others. Although, the source of healing isn't people, but instead the presence of Jesus in people. God can heal any brokenness in your life. The deep, dark, and dingy things buried in our souls can only be cleansed and healed by our loving heavenly Father.

- Exodus 14:14 "The Lord will fight for you, and you shall hold your peace."

We all face battles. We all face giants. But we all don't win. In order to prevail over the battles in life that we face, we must let God do the fighting. When we try to fight the devil in our own strength, we will lose every time. When we attempt to defeat temptations with our own willpower, we oftentimes will give into those enticements. However, when we submit to Christ and be still in his presence, supernatural power will begin to flow through us. We cannot attempt to do what only God can do.

Would you believe God today for his promises? The Bible is full of so many more promises as these are just a handful of foundational ones. If you will search out and study the Word of God, you will discover that our loving God has so many promises that pertain to all areas of our lives.

Believe God in a Real and Genuine Way

It has been said that religion is man's attempt to get to God; whereas a personal relationship with Jesus is God's attempt to get to man. God wants each of us to have a living, breathing, and active relationship with him. We have all met people who were classified as churchy, religious, and eccentric. At times, many of us have possibly been placed in one of those categories.

What I love about Jesus is that he is a genuine person who loves the world. I love that the Bible is not G-rated but real. The Bible pulls no punches when discussing the sins that men and women struggle with. If we are going to walk in God's blessing, we can't pretend to be something we are not. We have to be honest and real. God will never empower you to be someone else no matter how godly or wonderful that person might be. However, if you ask, God will empower you to be a supernatural you!

We need to make sure we don't try to act like we have it all together because first of all, that is a lie. None of us have it all together. Secondly, when we pretend like we have it all together people will see right through our facade. Oftentimes, when we share and acknowledge our limitations with others, we are able to connect on a deeper level with them. When we allow the love and power of God to shine through our failings, others can have hope. When we overcome great trials, people can see that there is a God and he will move in their lives. Being real is not a sign of weakness, but a sign of strength!

In order to live a life of blessing, we must believe God in a genuine way. Genuine means authentic. One of the greatest tests of our faith is how we act in private. When we honor God privately, it is a major indicator we are walking in a real relationship with him. If we honor God privately, we will have power to live for him publicly. When we serve people who can't pay us back, we are believing God in an authentic manner. When we decide to minister to people even when it is inconvenient, we are walking in the steps of Jesus. It is okay to help people who are affluent, but real ministry is serving, loving, and helping people who can't pay you back!

Your focus will determine your future. If your focus is on believing and trusting God in all areas of your life, you truly will live a blessed life. This world is full of distractions that the enemy would love to use to keep you from living a life of blessing. No denomination, pastor, or church can help you if you are not placing your faith in God. Believe God today!

WHAT TO LEAVE WITH

God wants you to live a life of blessing! In John 10:10 we read, "The thief does not come except to steal, and to kill, and to destroy. I have come that they may have life, and that they may have it more abundantly." The devil has a plan for you and so does Jesus. Your choices determine whose plan will succeed in your life!

If you want the devil's plan to succeed, trust yourself. If you want to miss out on the abundant life, try to do everything in your own power. If you want to be limited, rely on the wisdom and efforts of man. You will never get a blessed life by trying; you will only get a blessed life by trusting! You must totally and completely trust Jesus. Regardless of your circumstances, you have an opportunity to be blessed in each and every day.

If you want to live a life of blessing, step out in faith today. Believe God for his radical and outrageous blessings. Don't let your words or thoughts limit you. Don't let the words and thoughts of others limit you. If you want the abundant life, you need to live the obedient life! At the beginning of the book we defined what it means to live a life of blessing, which is doing what God has called you to do, being who God has called you to be, and having what God has called you to have. My desire is for you to live a life of blessing. I often pray this simple prayer and I hope you will pray it too:

"Lord, help me to do everything you want me to do, so I can be everything you want me to be, so I can have everything you want me to have. In Jesus name I pray, Amen."

Let me leave you with this final thought — The person who determines if you will live a life of blessing isn't your pastor or your friends, it's YOU! Please understand this truth - you don't get a blessed life by chance; you get a blessed life by choice. Living a life of blessing is a choice. Choose to live a blessed life today!

Books by Barry Young

30 Second Devotional

30 Second Devotional for First Responders

How to Have Victory in Life

How to Live a Life of Blessing

To learn more about Barry Young or Serving Pastors Ministries visit www.servingpastors.com